CW01651049

Brain Waves

Ancient Greece

Folens Publishers

John Corn

Acknowledgements

The author and publishers would like to thank the following for permission to reproduce photographs and other material:

Mary Evans Picture Library page 43: *The Battle of Salamis*

Editor: Ian Jenkins
Illustrations: Jane Bottomley
Layout artist: Suzanne Ward
Cover design: Hybert Design &Type

First published 1995 by Folens Limited, Dunstable and Dublin.
Folens Limited, Albert House, Apex Business Centre, Boscombe Road, Dunstable, LU5 4RL, England.

ISBN 1 85276757-X

Printed in Singapore by Craft Print

Contents

Introduction

The activity sheets in this book have been designed to provide a wide range of interesting and stimulating activities about Ancient Greece. The activities focus on:

- everyday life in Ancient Greece
- arts and architecture
- myths and legends
- the relationship of the Ancient Greeks with other peoples
- the legacy of Ancient Greek civilisation and its influence on the modern world.

The activity sheets have been designed to be practical, interesting and visually stimulating. The sheets are intended to support existing resources and should be used in the context of broader classroom discussion of the topics concerned. In this way, the activity sheets could extend and develop certain aspects of historical enquiry within the topic being studied. The topics do not need to be taught in sequence, but should be used selectively to stimulate, support and reinforce the teaching of history.

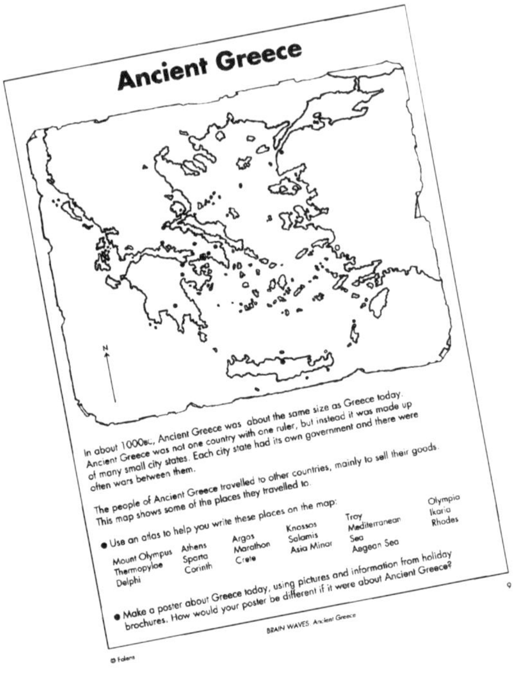

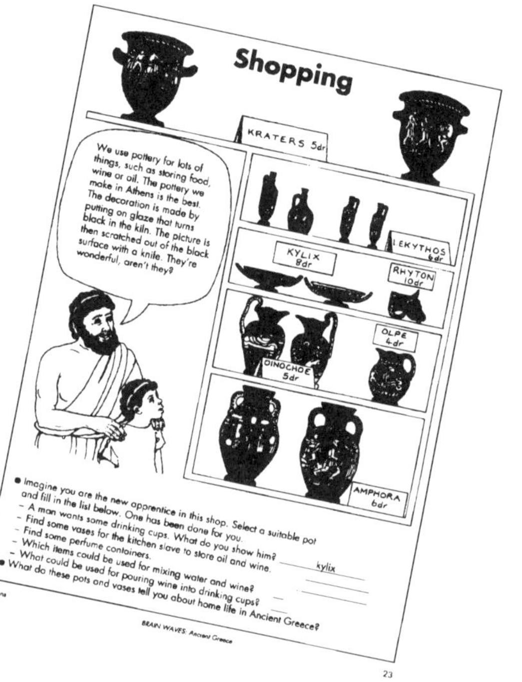

Each sheet has a specific focus within the topic concerned, and after a brief introduction the children are invited to explore a range of structured learning opportunities. These could be further developed in extension activities, such as classroom discussion, role play, and so on.

The questions and activities have been devised to:

- extend the children's knowledge and understanding of the issues introduced on the sheet in the context of the topic concerned
- assist the children in understanding history
- encourage the children to identify and use source material and to develop skills of historical enquiry.

The teachers' notes contain background information, along with ideas, suggestions and practical help. The notes include advice on potential pitfalls and problems, as well as details of materials required, extension activities, research opportunities and ideas for classroom displays.

Teachers' notes

Ancient Greece
The children will need:
- atlases
- holiday brochures featuring Greece
- a supply of A4 (or larger) plain paper for mounting the posters.

How it all began 1 and 2
These sheets could be enlarged on to A3 paper. The numbers 1 to 12 could be masked when photocopying to make the activity more challenging for more able children.

Athens and Sparta
Advertising posters or holiday posters could be made for Athens and Sparta as part of a large classroom display.

The Greeks at war
A good supply of reference books is essential for the activity. The children should be encouraged to investigate different interpretations of the same material. Story 1 is written from the point of view of the Spartans, while Story 2 is written from the Athenian point of view.

Citizens and slaves
Photocopy the sheet on to thin card. Reference books will be needed for the children to explore the social structure of a different time and place.

Slave labour
Records from 414BC show slave prices:
- small child – 72 drachma
- woman – 106–220 drachma
- man – 105–301 drachma

There are some opportunities for drama and role play about the slave market. For example, the children could design posters advertising the sale of some children and staff to help the schools budget! They could also discuss the advantages and disadvantages of slave labour, including a discussion about the points of view of both the slaves and the slave traders.

Pots of evidence
Discuss different types of evidence. Ask the children to list modern 'evidence' that a future archaeologist may find helpful when investigating their school. They could also investigate the idea of 'time capsules' and discuss one for their school. Broken modern pottery could be given to children as an introductory activity. The children could draw the pottery, reassemble it and consider its use.
The artefacts on the sheet are:
- amphora, used for storing wine
- drinking cup or kylix showing a charioteer
- statue of the Artemis, the goddess of wild animals and childbirth.

Greek trade
The children will require a map of the Mediterranean for reference. Ask them to study modern food labels to find out their country of origin. Discussions could include the need to buy some goods from abroad, which could be extended into a discussion of the need for trade in Ancient Greece. Trade was needed partly because of poor land and a rising population, which encouraged emigration and the establishment of new city states. Exports from Greece included olives, olive oil, pottery, silver and wine.

Trading places
This sheet should be used with the following sheet, 'Trading map'. Use a small notebook for the captain's log.

Trading map
The map should be photocopied and enlarged to A3 for clarity. The children could compare this map to a modern map of the same area.

Food and farming
Ask the children to compare the Ancient Greek diet with a modern one. Use an itemised supermarket receipt and mark off items that the Greeks may have produced. Reference books will be useful to complete a list of Greek foodstuffs.

Store detective
Use the sheet to help make 'shoe box' shops around an agora. The shops are a potter, a cobbler and an ironmonger.

Agora
This sheet should be photocopied on to card. The children should work in pairs to ensure that a large number and variety of stalls are made. Workshops of a more permanent nature would be found around the agora. Use this sheet in conjuction with 'Store detective'.

Shopping
Discuss the variety of pots and the ways in which they are decorated. The children could also speculate about their size and use, and consider the difference between facts and points of view.

A Greek urn
Colour photographs or pictures of pots and urns are a useful resource. The children could discuss colours, designs and techniques. The Greeks also used geometric designs: the children could investigate these and then use graph paper to practise their own designs.
The designs should be fairly specific (for example, a game, a lesson, or eating a meal) and should be coloured terracotta, black and white for display.

Houses and homes
The children could compare Ancient Greek building materials, layouts and functions with their modern equivalents. Reference books will be needed. Also, estate agents' leaflets and brochures are a useful source of information on modern house designs and functions.

Wall diggers
The items are:
- bedroom – earrings, powder pot, mirror
- gynaeceum – decorated vase, children's toy, baby's feeding bottle.
- andoron – jar for mixing water and wine, kylix, ram's head cup.

Going to school
Reference books will be needed. The children could compare Ancient Greek lessons with modern ones.

Play time
The information on this page could be used to make a pictorial time line about Ancient Greek toys. The children could then make a time line using their own toys and discuss the similarities and differences between the two.

Clothes
This sheet should be photocopied on to card. A prop made of card could be added to the figure to make it stand up. The children could discuss all aspects of clothes, including the similarities and differences between clothes worn by women, travelling men and workmen. Encourage the children to choose different periods, genders and occupations for their figures, so that a class time line on clothes can be produced. The children could write full descriptions to accompany each model. Extension activities could include dressing one of the children like one of the models.

Party time

Ask the children to investigate modern Greek food and drink. They could discuss a menu from a Greek restaurant and compare it with a menu from Ancient Greece. They could compile their own menu of Greek food, based on their likes and dislikes.

Hall of the gods

Make a large colour display showing the gods. The children could compare these gods with those of other periods and religions and draw up a chart to illustrate the similarities and differences.

The Parthenon

A simple model of the Parthenon could be made, using cardboard tubes for the pillars and squares of terracota-coloured card for the tiled roof. The children will need reference books while constructing their model.

Myths and legends

The story contains many errors for the children to spot and record. The main errors are:

- King Minos ruled Crete, not Sicily.
- The Minotaur had the head and horns of a bull, not a lion.
- Theseus promised to changed the sails of his ship from black to white, not blue.
- When Theseus returned to Athens, he forgot to change the colour of the sails. When King Aegeus saw the black sail he was convinced that Theseus had failed to kill the Minotaur. Aegeus killed himself in despair, not knowing that Theseus had succeeded and was still alive.

The children should work in pairs on the maze-building activity. The finished maze designs should be stuck on to backing paper and displayed, embellished with Greek designs and sketches of Theseus and the Minotaur. A good selection of reference books will be needed.

Heracles

This sheet should be enlarged to A3. A selection of reference books will be needed. The children should be familiar with the story of Heracles before beginning the game. The children could record their completion of a task by filling in a large class chart. Each child should show the teacher the answer to a question or a completed task and the teacher should judge if it has been completed satisfactorily. While some children are completing tasks, others should continue playing the game. This will add excitement and an element of competition to the game.

Philosophers

The answers are:

1. Aristotle
2. Socrates
3. Pythagoras
4. Hippocrates
5. Sophocles

Jason

The children should read the story of Jason and the Argonauts or Jason and the Golden Fleece before attempting the activities on this sheet. Extension activities could include:

- an investigation of modern versions of the story of Jason
- the children could write their own stories in the style of the Jason stories and produce a class booklet or display.

Theatre

Ask the children to make their own masks according to the dimensions on the sheet. The stick for the mask should be made of very thick card or an old ruler. The plots and scripts should be carefully planned by the children before being written in small groups. The plays could then be rehearsed before being performed in front of the whole class.

Making pots

Use tubs without a rim to produce the pots. A plate can be made in the same way as a pot:

- on the bottom of a plate, stick several layers of paper soaked with paste
- leave the layers to dry, remove the plate and paint and decorate the paper plate.

Brightly-painted plates make an excellent display. Each pot or plate should be accompanied by a description, an account of how it was used and perhaps a sketch of it being used.

Statues

The comments within the children's report could be wordprocessed and enlarged, and then cardboard rollers could be used to make an 'autocue', as used by television news readers. Good places to investigate statues are cathedrals, churches, war memorials, public buildings, parks and squares.

Music

This sheet should be photocopied on to card. The decorations should also be made on card. Modern equivalents of the instruments could be brought into the classroom for comparison, discussion and display.

Athens and Rome

Reference books about Athens and Rome are essential. The children could produce postcards about living in Rome or Athens, with a picture on one side and a written description of their experiences on the other side.

The Trojan War

The pictures are (clockwise from top left):

- based on a carving, about 600BC
- based on an eighteenth-century painting by Giovanni Tiepolo
- based on a modern reconstruction of the Trojan Horse in the 1980s.

The Battle of Salamis

Reference books will be needed for the children to complete the activities. Ask the children to use a large map of the area to locate the places and positions mentioned on the sheet.

Triremes

The game could be limited to 20 dice rolls per player to reduce the time taken to play the game. Encourage the children to investigate and discuss the role of triremes and their operational difficulties in times of war.

Olympia

Make a modern Olympics poster for your town or city, using contemporary Olympic events. The children could investigate the most recent Olympic Games.

The Greek alphabet

The game could be extended by giving each player a coloured card which could be played at any time. This card could change the order of play, make the next person miss a turn, or be used at any time to enable a player to use a letter that does not match the Greek letter. Extension activities could include translation of simple English words into Greek, or using numbers in a Greek bingo game. This will not be accurate but will encourage familiarisation with the language.

Democracy

The children should investigate further the information provided in each picture. They could explore in detail the issues raised in one or more of the pictures.

Greece – then and now

The children could work in small groups to produce a series of eye-catching displays for the classroom, each focusing on a specific area of life in ancient and modern Greece.

Ancient Greece

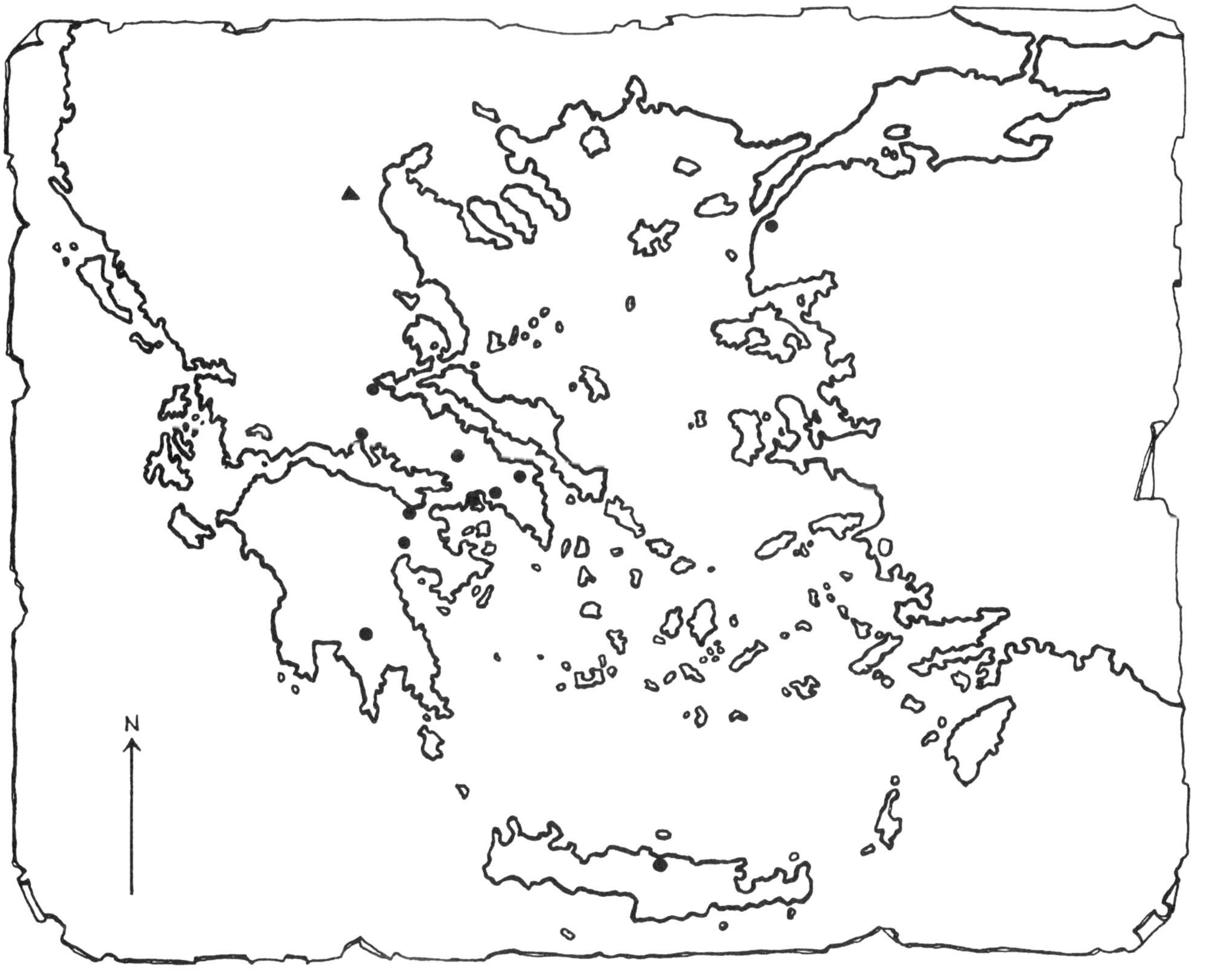

In about 1000BC, Ancient Greece was about the same size as Greece today. Ancient Greece was not one country with one ruler, but instead it was made up of many small city states. Each city state had its own government and there were often wars between them.

The people of Ancient Greece travelled to other countries, mainly to sell their goods. This map shows some of the places they travelled to.

- Use an atlas to help you write these places on the map:

Mount Olympus	Athens	Argos	Knossos	Troy	Olympia
Thermopylae	Sparta	Marathon	Salamis	Mediterranean Sea	Ikaria
Delphi	Corinth	Crete	Asia Minor	Aegean Sea	Rhodes

- Make a poster about Greece today, using pictures and information from holiday brochures. How would your poster be different if it were about Ancient Greece?

How it all began – 1

Ancient Greece lasted for about 2000 years.
During this time there were many changes in Greek life.
The pictures on these pages are mixed up.

2000–1600BC

1 The people of Crete built many palaces. This was the start of life in Ancient Greece.

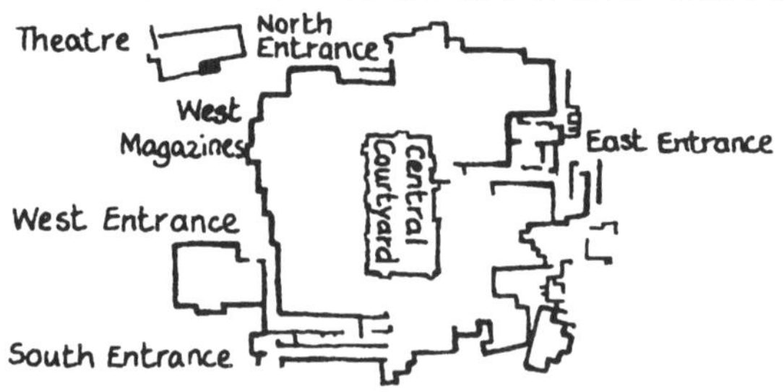

A plan of the Palace of Knossos.

Bronze Age

1150–950BC

4 People from Ancient Greece lived in Asia Minor, around the Black Sea and in the western Mediterranean.

A map of Ancient Greece.

Dark Age

336–323BC

11 Alexander the Great made Egypt and Persia part of the Greek Empire and spread Greek ideas all over the world.

Alexander the Great.

Classical Period

1600–1200BC

2 The Mycenaean people moved to Greece and brought new ideas about art and building. Some ideas came from Crete.

The gates at Mycenae.

Bronze Age

460–447BC

8 The first Peloponnesian War was fought between Sparta and Athens. This was the Golden Age of life in Ancient Greece.

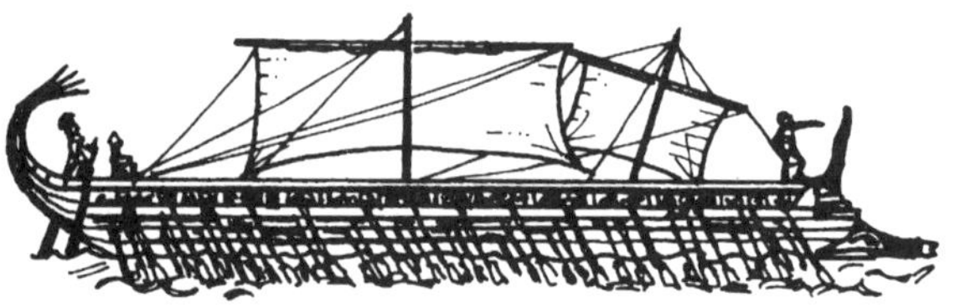

A Greek warship, called a trireme.

Classical Period

431–404BC

10 The Great Peloponnesian War. The people of Athens were defeated by Sparta.

Soldiers fighting during the war.

Classical Period

How it all began – 2

- Cut out the pictures and put them in the correct order.
  Then join the time line together to make a display.
- Which part of the time line shows the most changes to life in Ancient Greece?
- What do you think was the most important change? Why?

495–425BC

7 The government of Ancient Greece changed. People had more freedom and elections were held.

Voting tokens from a court in Ancient Greece. The token with a hole means 'guilty'. The token without a hole means 'not guilty'.

Classical Period

776–479BC

6 The people of Athens won a battle with the Persians at Marathon in 490BC. They won another battle in 479BC.

A messenger running to Athens to tell of the victory at Marathon.

Archaic Period

447BC

9 The people of Athens begin building the Parthenon.

The Parthenon as it looks today.

Classical Period

950–776BC

5 The first Olympic Games was held in 776BC.

Athletes at the first Olympic Games.

Archaic Period

1200BC

3 A war was fought between Mycenae and the city of Troy.

The Trojan horse.

Bronze Age

146BC

12 The end of the Greek Empire. Greece became part of the Roman Empire.

All parts of Greek life were taken over by the Romans, such as the coins that were used.

Hellenistic Period

Athens and Sparta

Ancient Greece was not one country with one ruler. It was made up of many small city states. Each city state (called *polis* in Greek) had its own laws and government. There was often fighting between the states.

The two most important city states were Athens, which was famous for its arts and education, and Sparta, which was famous for its powerful army. There was great rivalry between Athens and Sparta.

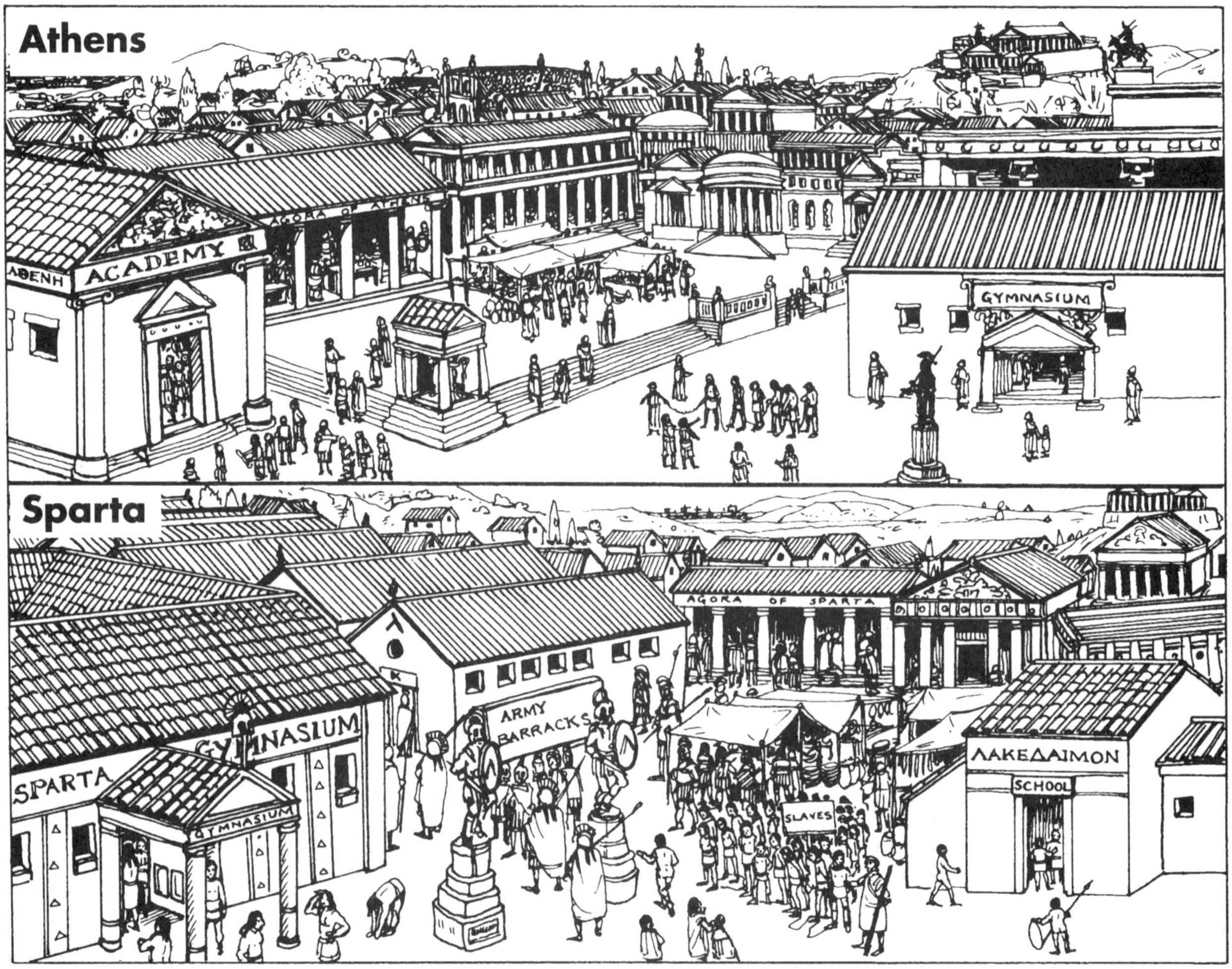

- Make a chart showing the similarities and differences between Athens and Sparta.
- Using the information on this page, write three facts and three points of view that a citizen for each place might say about their city.
- Which city would you prefer to live in. Why?
  Give reasons for your answer.

The Greeks at war

The Peloponnesian War was fought between Athens and Sparta, from 431BC to 404BC. Some stories of the war give different ideas about what happened.

The Peloponnesian War – Story 1

The Peloponnesian War was fought between Athens and Sparta. The war began when the army of Athens fought a terrible battle with Corinth, a city state that was friendly with Sparta. The people of Sparta wanted to help their friends, so they invaded Athens in 431BC.

At first, Athens began to win the war. The Athenian navy was lucky to win a sea battle at Naupactus in 429BC.

However, the Spartan army won a great battle in 422BC, when the leader of Athens was killed. From then on, the Spartans won many battles until Athens was forced to give up in 404BC. Sparta became the most important city state in Ancient Greece.

The Peloponnesian War – Story 2

The Peloponnesian War was fought between Athens and Sparta. The war began because the Spartans were rebellious people who wanted to control all of Greece. The Spartan army invaded Athens in 431BC.

Athens quickly began to win the war. The army of Athens won a great battle at Naupactus in 429BC.

However, when the Spartans murdered the leader of Athens in 422BC, Sparta began to win the war. The people of Athens were forced to give up in 404BC, but Athens was still an important city state.

- Read carefully the two stories about the war.
- Draw and complete a chart to show the facts and the points of view in each story.
- Write the story in your own words. Add a headline and pictures.

	fact	point of view
story 1	1. 2.	1. 2.
story 2	1. 2.	1. 2.

Citizens and slaves

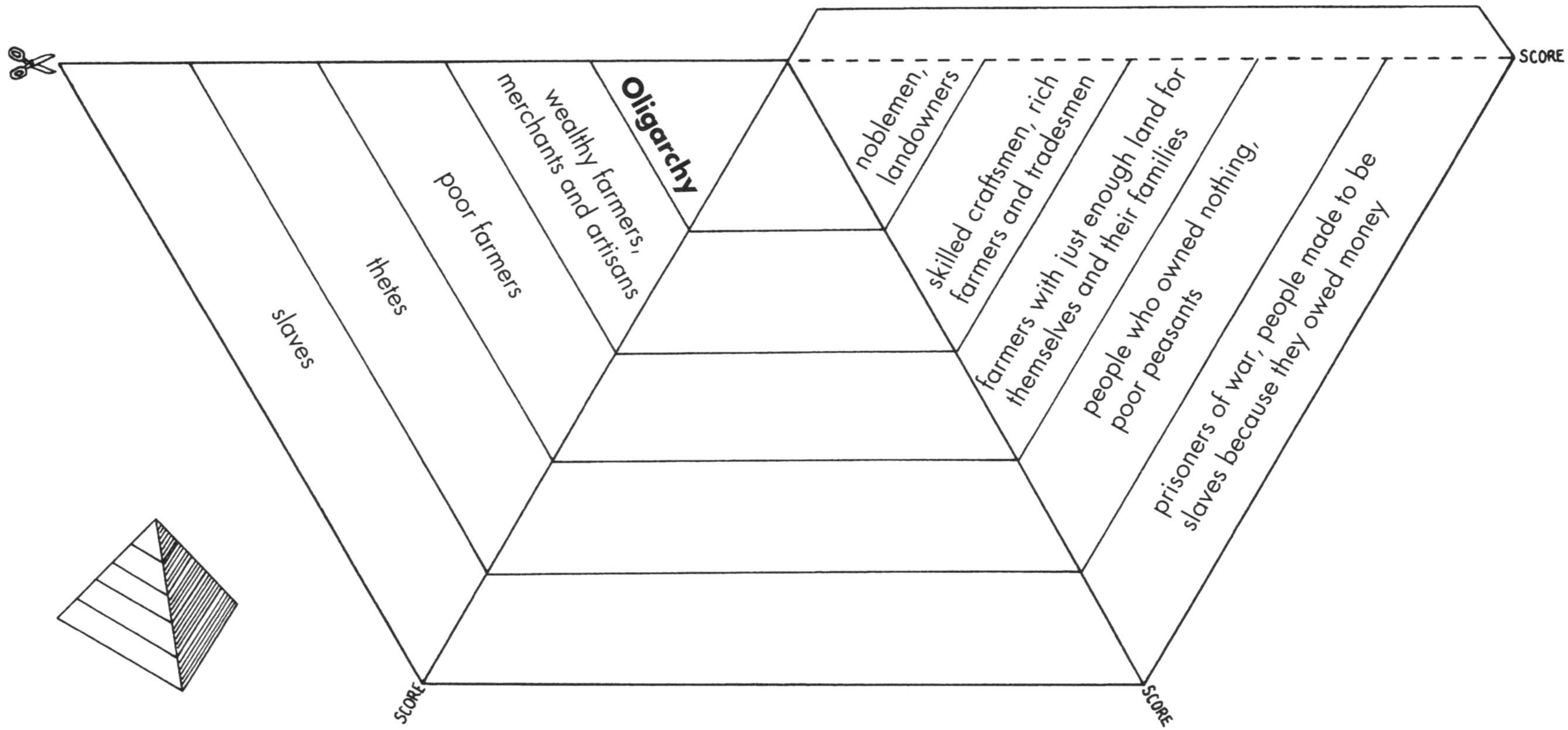

In the city states of Ancient Greece, people were divided into groups, each with certain rights and duties. Oligarchy means 'rule by a small group', which means that a small group of rich and powerful men ruled the state. The citizens were groups of wealthy farmers, merchants and artisans, as well as poor farmers and poor peasants. Slaves were at the bottom of the system. They were owned by the people they worked for and they had very few rights.

- The pyramid diagram on this page shows the different social groups in Ancient Greece. In the blank space for each group, draw and colour a picture or diagram.
- Mount the diagram on to card, cut it out and make it into a pyramid.
- Find out about society in a different time and place, for example Roman Britain. Make another pyramid and write a list of the similarities and differences that you discover between this society and Ancient Greece.

Slave labour

In Athens most of the hard and dirty work was done by slaves. Many slaves worked in the houses of wealthy citizens. Other slaves worked in workshops and the really unlucky slaves worked down the mines. I could sell slaves for a lot of money, but the price depended on how educated, skilled and beautiful the slave was.

sold to: ....

sold to: ....

sold to: ....

sold to: ....

mistress

mine owner

older mistress

workshop owner

- Link each slave to their new owner by writing the name of the owner beneath each picture.
- Look carefully at each of the slaves and write a list to describe the kind of job that each slave does.
- Imagine that you want to buy a new slave. Write a list of questions that you might want to ask before buying.

Pots of evidence

To help us understand the past we need evidence. An important kind of evidence is artefacts, tools and equipment that were used by people in their everyday life. These damaged artefacts were found on the site of a house in Athens. The rulers show the size of each artefact.

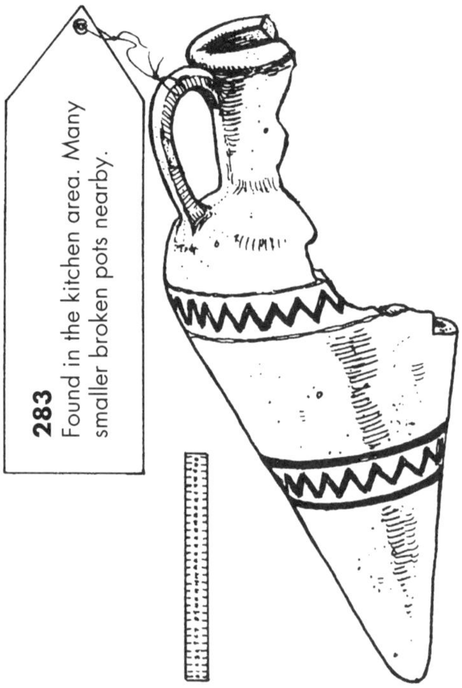

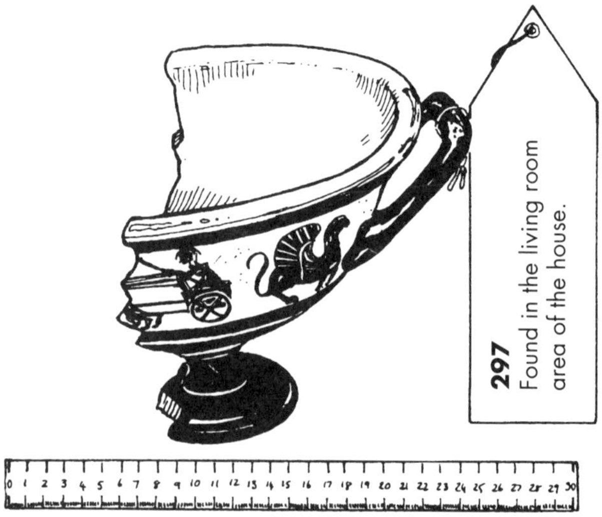

- Complete a chart for each artefact.

Excavation: the house of Stavros in Athens			
Number	**Size (cm)**	**Description**	**Use**
283			

- Cut out each artefact with its tag.
- Colour it and stick on a piece of paper. Draw the outline of the missing piece or pieces. What do you think each artefact would have been used for?
- What do the artefacts tell you about Stavros' house in Athens?

Greek trade

Symbol	Import	From (city states)
	Grain	Cyrene Naucratis Olbia Selinus
	Slaves	Sinope
	Dyes	Al Mina
	Silphium (a herb used for food and medicine)	Cyrene
	Timber	Odesseus Histria
	Wine	Masillia Rhodes
	Hides	Olbia Cyrene Neapolis
	Wool	Cyrene
	Fish	Black Sea
	Papyrus	Naucratis

Cargo ships at a busy harbour.

The Ancient Greeks had to find a way of taking food to the people of Athens. Mainland Greece was very mountainous, which made travelling difficult and meant that wheat, which was used to make bread, was hard to grow. Most grain was brought to Athens by ship from the city states. Other goods were brought to Athens in this way.

- Look carefully at the chart. Draw a symbol for each of the items imported into Athens.
- Choose one of the imports from the chart, then do some research and explain why it came from that area.
- Find out what Athens sold to the city states.

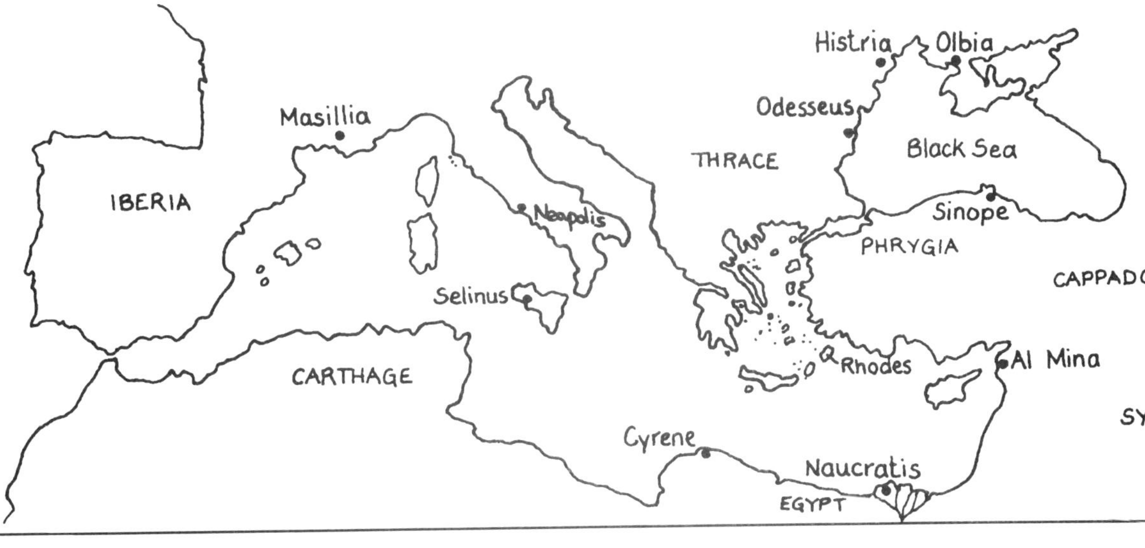

Trading places

Cargo ships in Ancient Greece were about 30 metres long with a square sail on a single mast. Ships sailed during the day between April and September and could cover about 75km a day. They sailed all around the Mediterranean, delivering and collecting goods from the ports.

This is a game for two players. Imagine that you own a ship that delivers and collects goods around the eastern Mediterranean Sea. The object of the game is to move across the board, collecting and delivering goods.

- You will need two counters, nine playing cards each, a dice and a ruler.
- Place the 'collect' cards on the map, next to the correct city state.
- Each player starts the game at Piraeus with five 'deliver' cards.
- The number rolled on the dice shows how far a player can move across the board in centimetres. Your ship can move in any direction, but you have to visit each port to finish the game.
- When you reach a port, you must either collect a card or deliver one. **Remember** – your ship can carry only five cards at a time or it will sink, so you must plan your route carefully.
- If you roll a **1**, roll the dice again.
  - If you throw **1** again, bad weather – sail back to last port.
  - If you throw **3**, cargo overboard – miss a turn.
  - If you throw **5**, calm weather – miss a turn.
- If your ship lands on a shaded area, you have been attacked by pirates. Miss a turn and give up two cards.
- The winner is the first player to get back to Piraeus with their four 'collect' cards.

DELIVER **Rhodes** 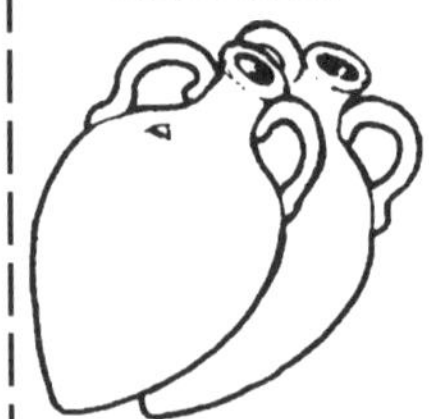 **wine**	COLLECT **Lesbos**  **silver**	DELIVER **Andros**  **olives**
DELIVER **Salamis**  **pottery**	DELIVER **Knossos**  **cloth**	COLLECT **Cyrene**  **grain**
COLLECT **Naucratis** 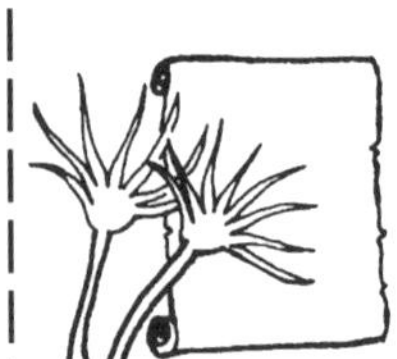 **papyrus**	DELIVER **Perge**  **olive oil**	COLLECT **Al Mina**  **dyes**

- When you have finished the game, write a captain's log to give an account of your journey and the goods you carried.

Trading map

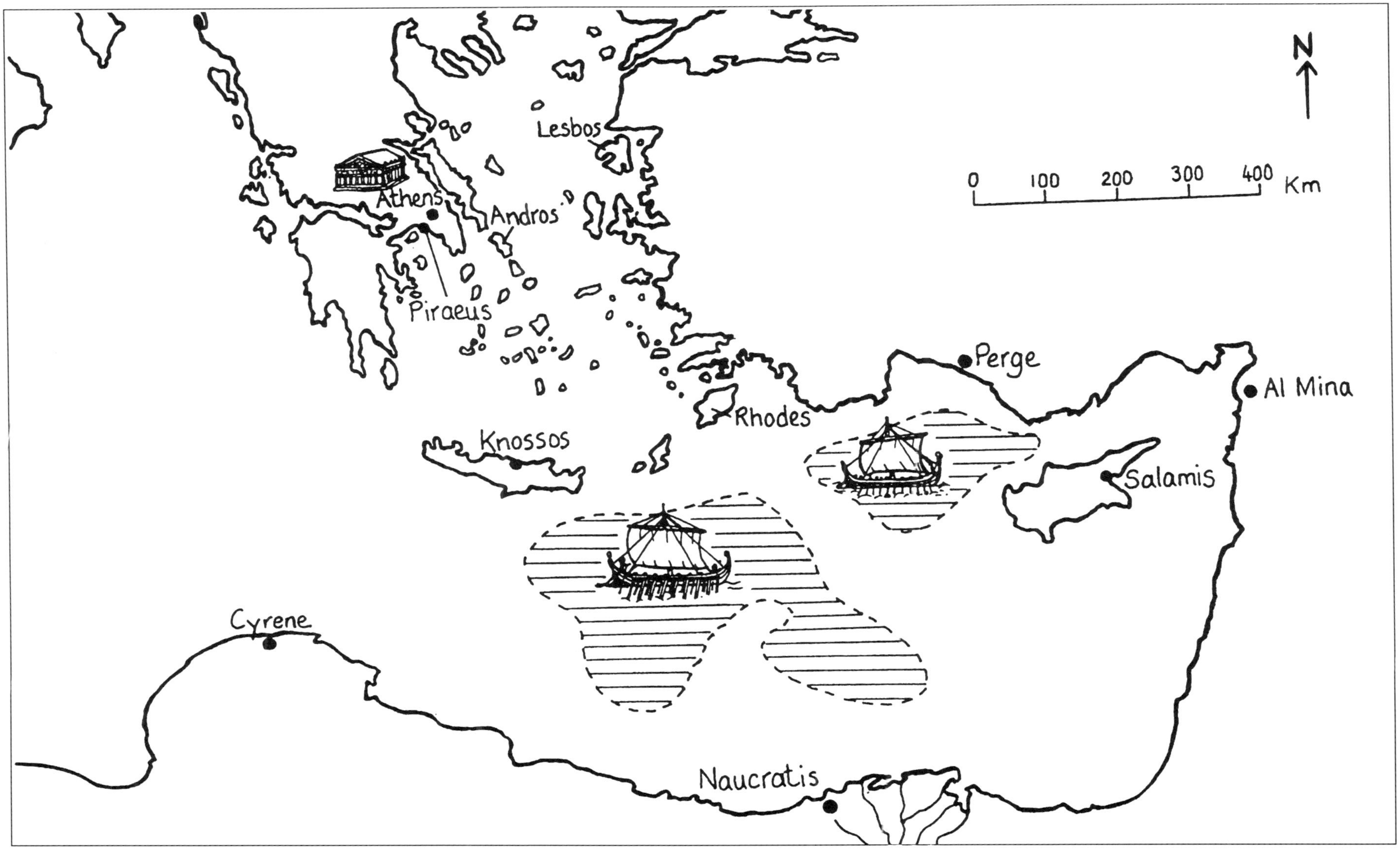
N
0
100
200
300
400
Km
Lesbos
Athens
Andros
Piraeus
Knossos
Rhodes
Perge
Al Mina
Salamis
Cyrene
Naucratis

Food and farming

The diet of the Ancient Greeks was very simple compared to ours.
They ate bread, cheese and vegetables, and fish if they lived near the coast.
Meat was expensive, so only wealthy people could afford to eat it.
Many people grew food of their own and kept their own animals.

- Look carefully at the picture and write a list of the different kinds of food being produced.
- From your list, choose the items of food that we still eat today.
- Find out about some other items of food that were eaten in Ancient Greece.
  Draw your own pictures.

Store detective

In Ancient Greece, everyday goods were made in small workshops. These included carpenters, potters and metal workers. The workshops were run by the owner, perhaps with an apprentice and a few slaves.

- Work out what is happening in each of the workshops. Write a description in the chart and use it to work out what each sign says.
- Each workshop contains the owner, a slave and a shopper. Work out who is who and label them.
- Imagine you are walking past these workshops along one side of the Agora, or market place. Describe the sounds and smells coming from each workshop.

Shop name	**Description**

Agora

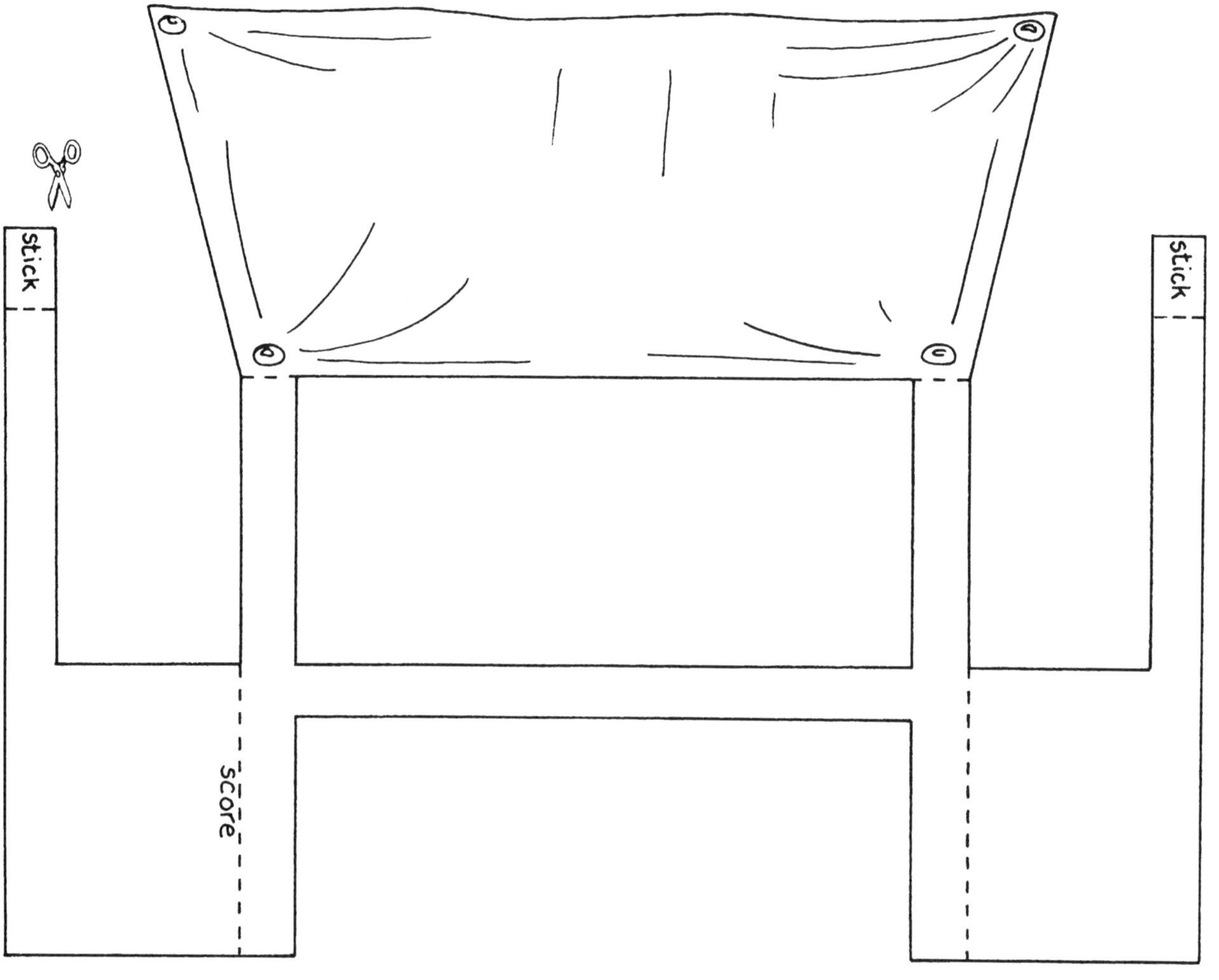

In the middle of every city in Ancient Greece was the 'agora' or market place. People visited the agora to buy food and household goods. It was a busy and noisy place.

- Cut out the plan above and make a stall. Choose something from this list to sell at the stall:
  - bread
  - cheese
  - olives and olive oil
  - honey
  - cloth
  - fish
  - fruit and vegetables
  - pottery
  - nuts
  - spices.
- In a group, make stalls for each of these goods and then design and make an agora containing the stalls. You could add a Greek statue in the centre.

Shopping

- Imagine you are the new apprentice in this shop. Select a suitable pot and fill in the list below. One has been done for you.
  - A man wants some drinking cups. What do you show him? kylix
  - Find some vases for the kitchen slave to store oil and wine. ____________
  - Find some perfume containers. ____________
  - Which items could be used for mixing water and wine? ____________
  - What could be used for pouring wine into drinking cups? ____________
- What do these pots and vases tell you about home life in Ancient Greece?

A Greek urn

Greek pottery was highly decorated. Pottery such as vases and urns are an important source of evidence because many of them show scenes of everyday life in Ancient Greece. Some pottery shows pictures that tell the stories of Greek myths and legends.

- What do you think this urn might have been used for?
- Describe what you think is happening in the picture on the urn. Compare your description with a friend's.
- The picture comes from the story of Odysseus. Find out more about the story and discuss how well you think the urn shows this part of the story.
- Draw your own urn and decorate it to show a scene from your favourite story. When you have finished, colour the picture using black and terracotta.
- Write a list of similarities and differences between the urn on this page and your urn.

Houses and homes

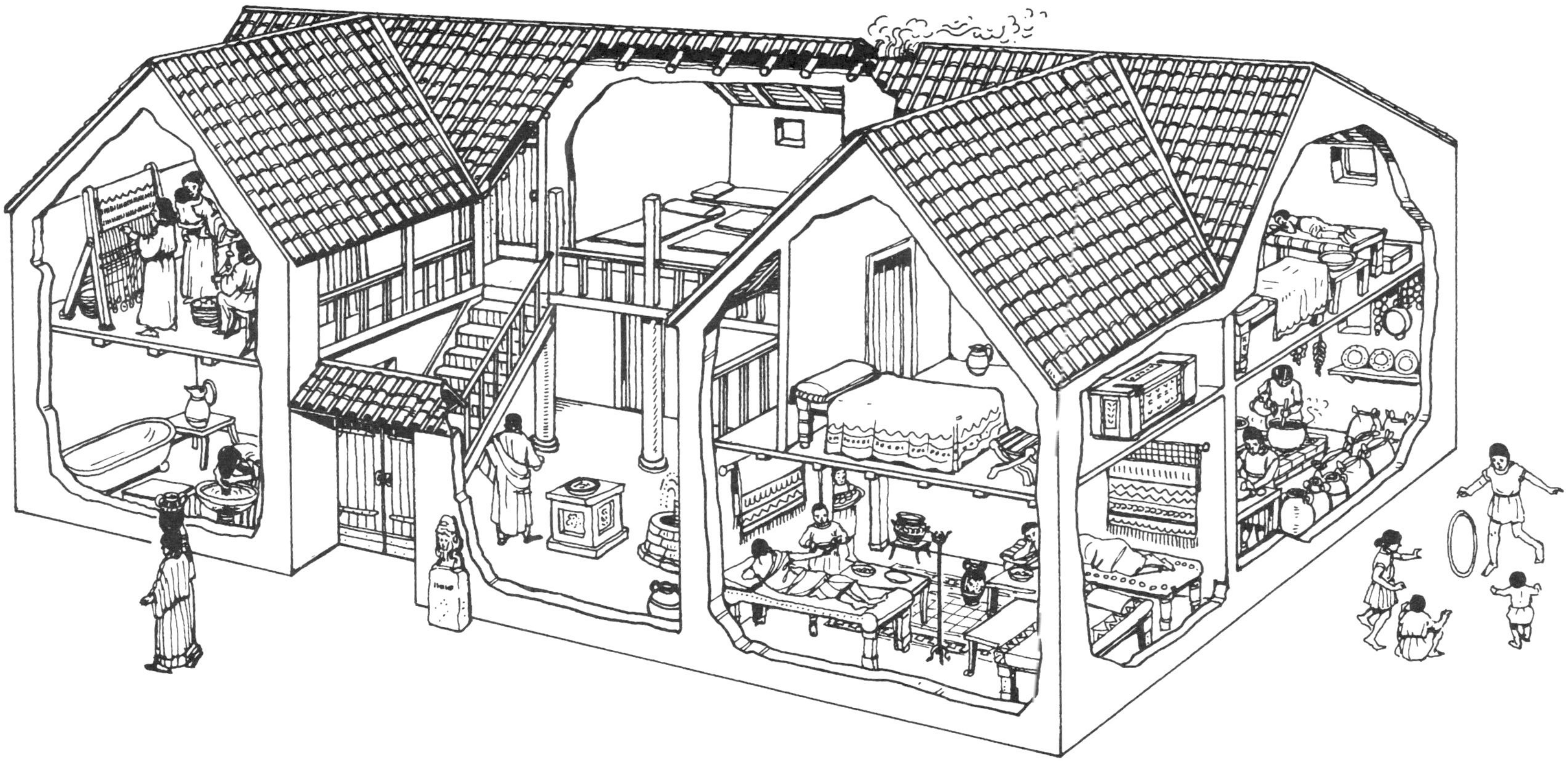

Houses in Ancient Greece were built from sun-baked mud brick. They had timber supports and a roof made from tiles or thatch. Most homes were very simple, but the homes of wealthy people had many rooms, often on two floors around a courtyard.

room labels

courtyard	
gynaeceum (room for women)	andoron (room for men)
bathroom	bedroom
slaves' room	kitchen

- Imagine visiting a house in Ancient Greece, like the one in the picture. Walk around the house. Label each room when you come to it and describe what you see, what is happening, the sounds and the smells.
- Write about who might have used each room, when they might have used it and why.
- Draw a picture like this to show your house. Compare it to the Ancient Greek house and write a list of what has changed about houses and what has stayed the same.

Wall diggers

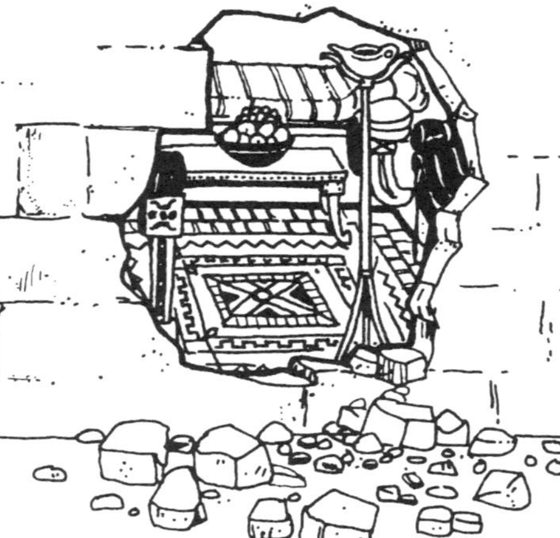

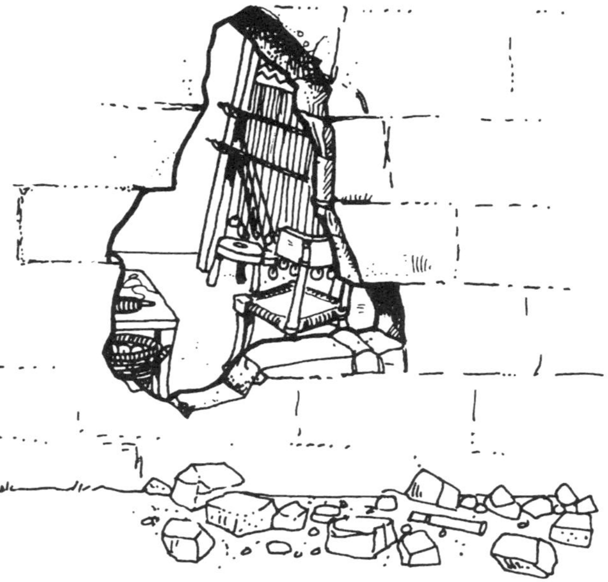

Houses in Ancient Greece were easy to burgle. The walls were made out of soft brick and so 'wall diggers' could easily break their way in and steal what they wanted.

objects taken from the rooms		
 children's toy	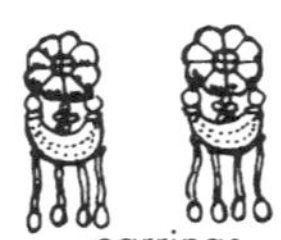 earrings	 mirror
 drinking cup called a 'kylix'	 jar to mix water and wine	 baby's feeding bottle
 powder pot for make-up	 vase showing baby on potty	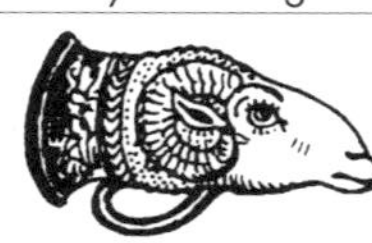 cup shaped as a ram's head

- Look carefully at the picture above and then look at the collection of objects that have been taken from the rooms.
- Complete this chart to show which item could have been taken from which room. Draw a picture of the items in the correct place.

room	items		
bedroom			
gynaeceum (room for women)			
andoron (room for men)			

- Do you think any of these items would be found in a house today? If so, choose one and draw a picture to show what it looks like today.

Going to school

In Ancient Greece children were educated to prepare them for adult life. Education was different in each city state. In Athens, boys were sent to school and girls were taught at home.

In the afternoons the boys play sports to make them strong for the army. Boys practise wrestling, boxing, running, discus and javelin.

Most girls did not go to school, although some had private tutors at home. Many girls were taught by their mothers about their role in marriage and how to run their home.
Most girls were married at the age of 15.
In some city states, girls were also taught about physical fitness.

Girls' Timetable
spinning weaving cooking fetching water buying food running a home

- Imagine that you visited a school in Athens in 462BC. Write a report on the school and say whether you think it is a good or bad school, or somewhere in between.
- Complete a chart to show the similarities and differences between education for boys and girls in Ancient Greece.

Similarities	Differences
1. 2. 3.	1. 2. 3.

- Think about the way you are taught in your school. How is it different from schools in Ancient Greece? How is it similar?

Play time

Greek children had many toys and games. We still have many of these toys and games today.

- Look at the pictures. Describe what is shown in each picture.
- What do you think the toys and games are made from? Describe how you think they were used.
- Which toys or games do you think would be used by very young children and which by older children? Write the letters in order, starting with the toy or game for the youngest child.
- Find some pictures of modern toys and games.
- Arrange the pictures in order, starting with the toy or game for a young child.
- Write a list of the similarities and differences between modern toys and games and those from Ancient Greece.

A a game called 'knucklebones'

B a board game

C a toy horse

D a baby's rattle

E children playing 'chariots'

F a spinning top

G children on a swing

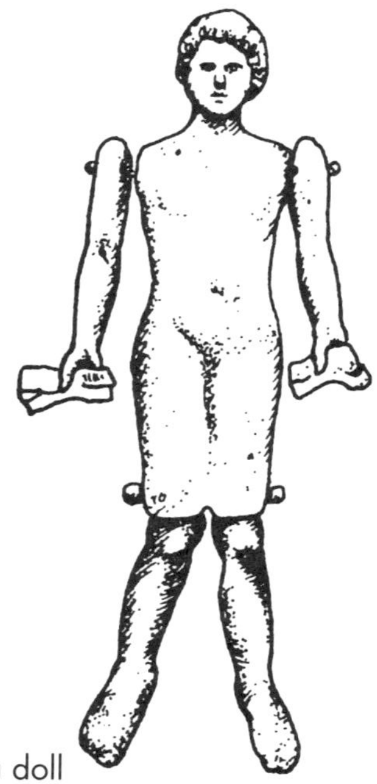
H a doll

Clothes

The main type of clothing in Ancient Greece was the 'chiton'. This was a large piece of woollen cloth draped over the shoulders and around the waist, held up with a belt made from leather or cord.

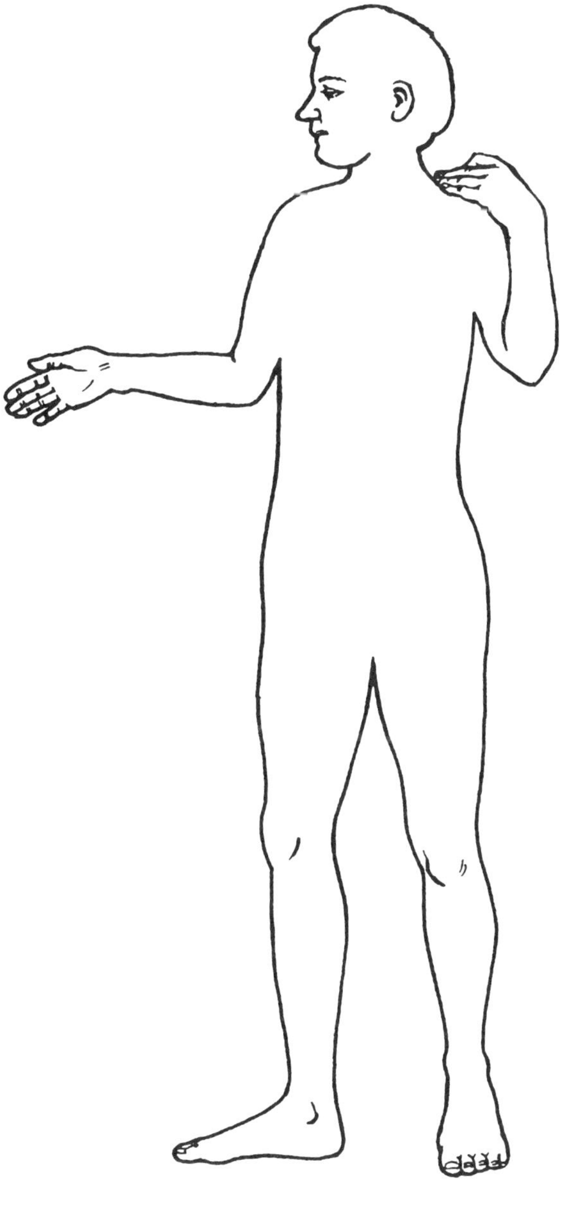

Fact file

Men and boys:

- short chitons above the knee, usually white, except for workmen who wore dark colours so that the dirt did not show
- hats: travelling men wore a wide-brimmed hat made of wool, fox fur or straw
- hair: long, usually tied back, and a beard
- footwear: sandals, or boots in the country.

Women and girls:

- clothes: long chitons (ankle length or longer), with brooches to keep the chiton in place and bracelets as jewellery
- hats: cloaks pulled over their heads or a veil, because a suntan was thought unattractive
- hair: long, usually tied back
- footwear: sandals, or boots in the country.

- Design some clothes that might have been worn in Ancient Greece. Use your design to dress the model.
- Describe how clothes for men and women were different.
- Write a list to show some differences between clothes in Ancient Greece and clothes today. Is anything the same?

Party time

The people of Ancient Greece loved food and wine. For many people, the main meal of the day was in the evening, when big dinner parties were often held. After several courses they would have a 'symposium' (a drinking party) and perhaps eat 'sweetmeats' (sweets or cakes).

sesame seeds

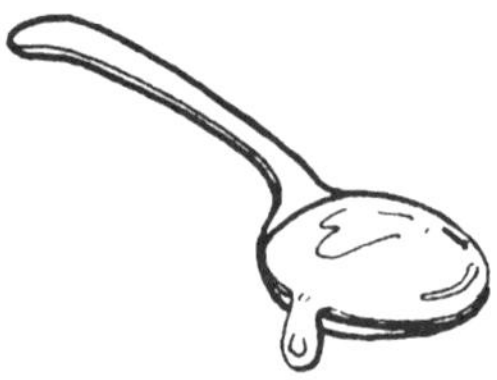

honey

chopped dates, figs and nuts

- Make your own sweetmeats that might have been eaten at an Ancient Greek party. This is what you will need:
  - 100g of sesame seeds
  - 5 tablespoons of honey
  - 100g of chopped dates, figs and nuts

- Put all of the ingredients into a saucepan on a low heat. Let the mixture simmer for about 15 minutes, stirring all the time.
- Take the saucepan off the heat and keep stirring until the mixture is cool. Using clean hands, take some of the mixture from the saucepan and roll it into a small ball. Keep making the balls until you run out of mixture.
- Arrange your sweetmeats on a small plate, ready to serve.

simmer the mixture

roll the mixture into balls

- Find out more about parties in Ancient Greece.
  Make a display to show a party and the kind of food and drink there.

Hall of the gods

The Ancient Greeks believed that their gods and goddesses lived on Mount Olympus, from where they looked down on everyone. There were 12 gods and goddesses and each of them controlled a different part of life. Each one could bring good luck to those that pleased them and bad luck to those who offended them. These pictures show five of the gods and goddesses.

Zeus

Poseidon

Aphrodite

Ares

Hades

- Find out about these gods and goddesses and write a description of each of them.
- Draw and colour a suitable background for each of the gods and goddesses on this page.
- Write a list of the Ancient Greek gods and goddesses that are not shown here. Draw a picture of each of them.
- Zeus was the king of the gods. Write the names of all of the gods on cards and arrange them in order of importance. Explain why you have arranged them in this order.

The Parthenon

The Greeks built many temples to please their gods and goddesses. The Acropolis of Athens was the highest part of the city and contained some of the finest temples in Ancient Greece. One of these temples was the Parthenon.

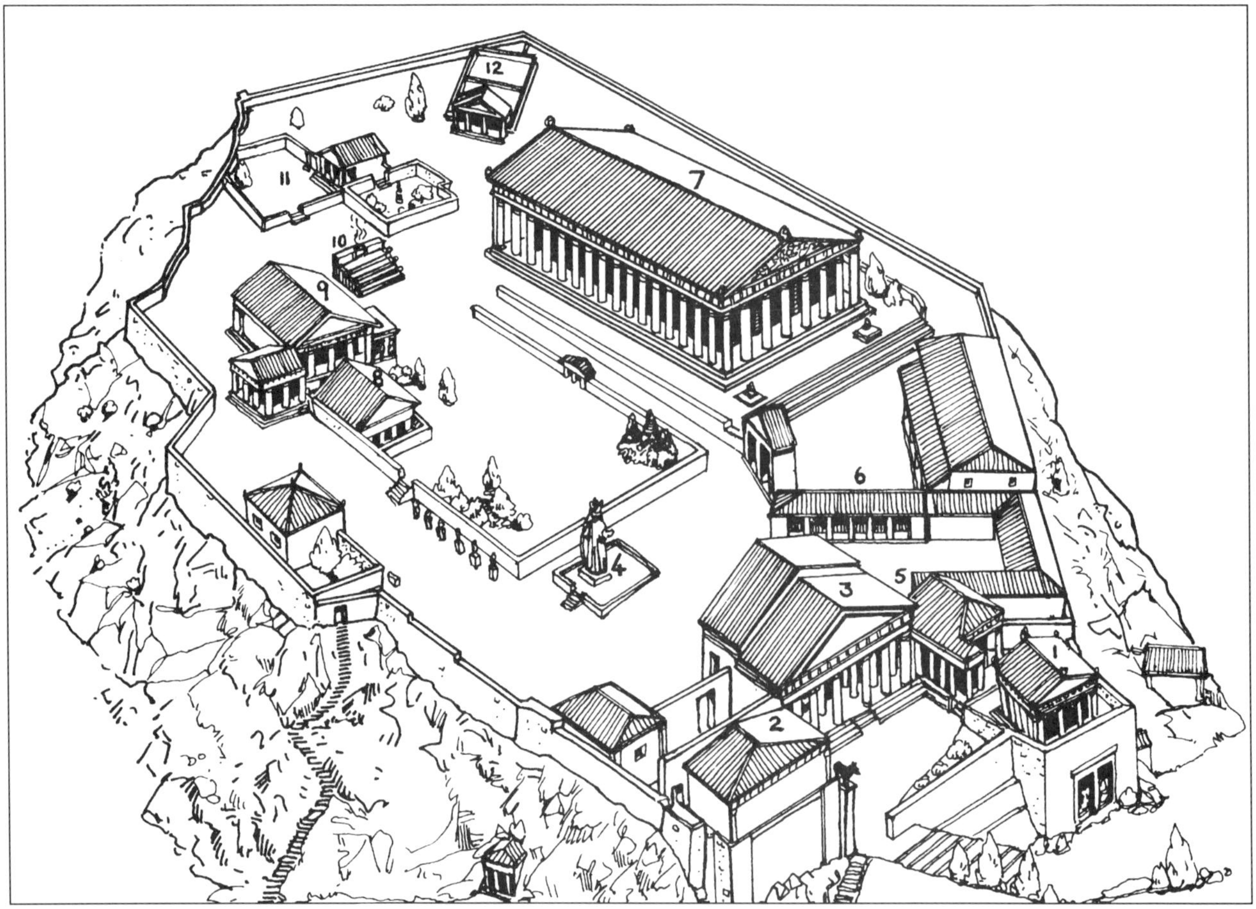

Key

1. Temple of Athena Nike
2. Gallery of Paintings
3. 'Propylaea' (great entrance)
4. Bronze statue of Athena
5. Sanctuary of Artemis Brauronia
6. The chalkoteki
7. The Parthenon
8. Temple of Pandroses
9. The Erechtheum temple
10. Altar of Athena
11. Enclosure of Zeus, Polieus and Bukoleion, where wheat, barley and a sacred ox were offered to the gods and goddesses
12. Temple of Pandion

The Greeks began building the Parthenon in 447BC. It took 15 years to build. Inside stood a huge gold and ivory statue to Athena. Around the outside of the building was a carved marble frieze showing 192 Centaurs (creatures that were half man, half horse).

- How many temples were on the Acropolis?
- Draw a plan of the Acropolis and label it.
- Find out more about the Parthenon. Describe how it was designed and built.
- What are the Elgin Marbles? Why are they important?

Myths and legends

The Ancient Greeks told many stories. Some of the stories were based on real events and people. These are called legends. Some of the stories were about religious beliefs and gods or goddesses. These are called myths.

Theseus and the Minotaur

Underneath the Palace of Knossos, the home of King Minos of Sicily, was a maze. In the maze lived a terrible monster called the Minotaur. It had the head and horns of a lion and the body of a man. It ate people.

King Minos' son was killed in Athens. The king blamed the Athenians and sent warships to attack them. King Aegeus of Athens begged for peace. King Minos agreed, on condition that Athens sent six boys and six girls to be fed to the Minotaur every seven years. King Aegeus' son, Theseus, wanted to go and kill the Minotaur. "When I come home," he said, "I will change the colour of the sail on my ship from black to blue to show you I have been successful."

King Minos' daughter Ariadne fell in love with Theseus and told him the secrets of the maze. She gave him a knife to kill the Minotaur and a ball of wool to unroll as he entered the maze and follow to get out again. Theseus went alone, deep into the maze. He soon met the Minotaur and plunged the knife deep into its neck, killing it instantly. When Theseus returned to Athens he changed the sail of his ship from black to blue. He was greeted by his father after a hero's welcome.

- This story of Theseus and the Minotaur contains some errors.
  Check this version of the story with another and highlight any errors you find.
- Is this a myth or a legend? Give reasons for your answer.
- Design a maze that could be used to help tell the story.
- Draw a picture of Theseus and the Minotaur and use it with your maze to make a display.

Heracles

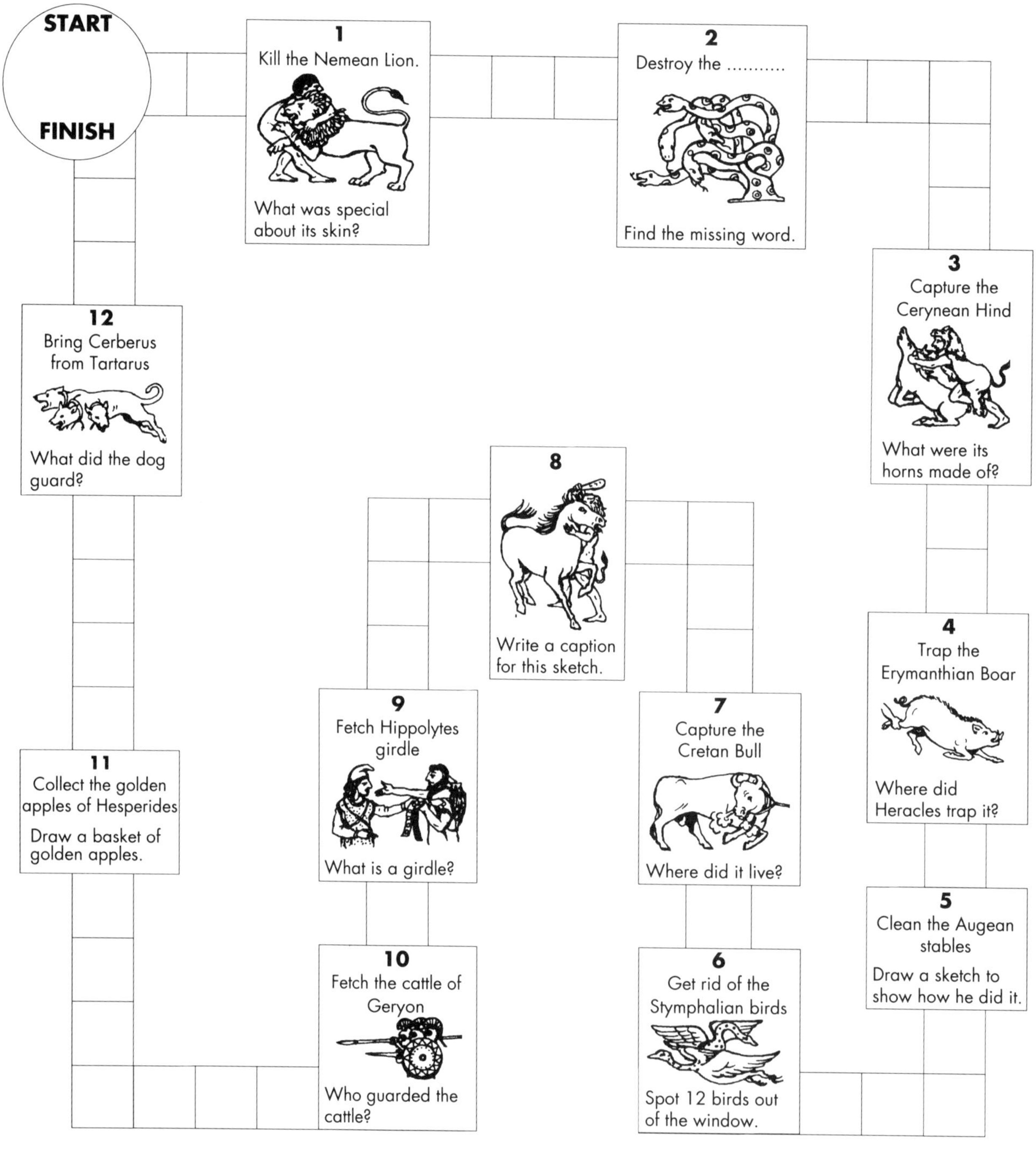

- This is a game for four players. Each player will need a counter and some reference books.
- The first player to roll a six with the die starts the game. Each player moves around the board and completes each task. The winner is the first player to complete all of the tasks and reach the finish.
- If you reach the finish without completing all of the tasks, go round again and complete those you have missed.
- If you get an answer wrong, miss a turn and then try again.

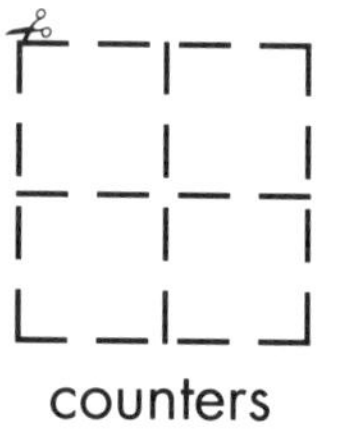
counters

Philosophers

The Ancient Greeks were very interested in the world around them and how it worked. Greek thinkers studied many subjects, such as astronomy, medicine and mathematics. These people were called philosophers. Most philosophers lived in Athens.

Aristotle

1. One of the first great philosophers of Ancient Greece. He questioned common beliefs in order to find new ideas and truths.

2. He believed that everyone should be treated equally and that every citizen should take part in government.

Socrates

3. He was born on the island of Samos. He believed that the key to the world lay in mathematics.

Pythagoras

Hippocrates

4. Born on the island of Kos, he wrote books on medical topics called Corpus. Modern doctors base their work on him and his teaching.

5. He became a great dramatist and wrote over 130 plays, including **Antigone**, **Electra** *and* **Oedipus Rex.**

Sophocles

- What does the word 'philosopher' mean?
- Read the information on this page and look at the pictures. Draw a line between the philosopher and his ideas.
- Choose one of the philosophers. Research his ideas and write about some of them.

Jason

One of the most famous Greek myths is that of Jason and the Golden Fleece.

- Write these captions in the empty boxes:
  - Jason sailed past the Clashing Rocks.
  - Jason built a ship call the Argo. His crew were called the Argonauts.
- Use the information in the pictures to write in the empty speech bubbles.
- Do some research and draw the missing pictures, then draw more to complete the story.

Theatre

The theatre was an important part of Ancient Greek life and most cities had an amphitheatre where plays were performed. Performances would last most of the day and during them actors wore large masks to show their characters. The plays could be tragedies or comedies.

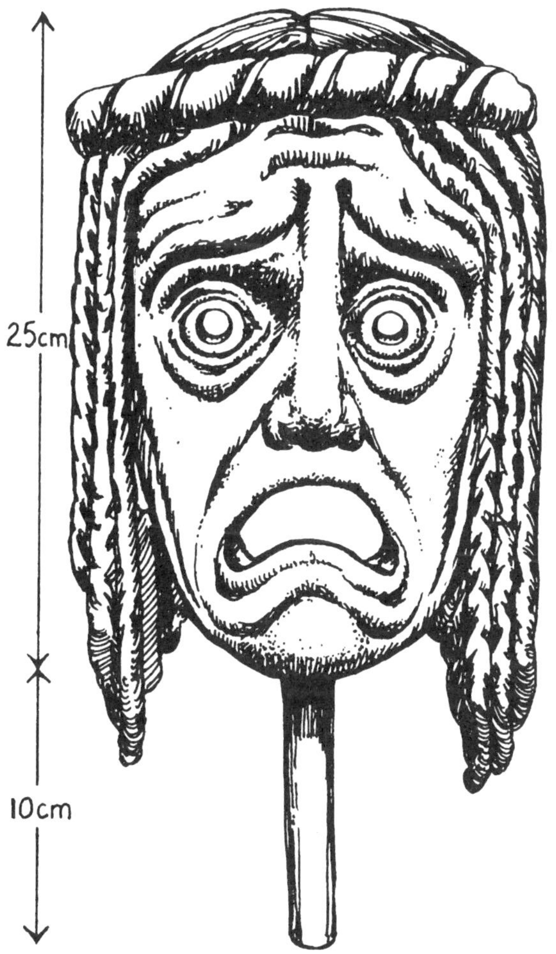

- Write a word beneath each mask to describe the feeling it shows.
- What are 'tragedies' and 'comedies'?
- Find out what an amphitheatre looked like. Why do you think they were this shape?
- Write a short play. Here are some ideas:

1
Heracles feels very guilty after killing his family. He is told to go as a slave to King Eurystheus who sets Heracles 12 tasks. He must complete them all if he is to become immortal.

2
Daedalus, an inventor, and his son Icarus plan to escape from King Minos. They devise a plan to escape using wings made with wax and feathers. Daedalus warns Icarus not to fly too close to the sun. Icarus ignores him.

3
Zeus punishes humanity for accepting the gift of fire. Hephaestos creates a woman, Pandora, who takes a jar from Zeus to Epimethius. She is told not to open the jar. She does and out fly the evils of the world, except hope.

- Make a mask to use in your play, like the one shown here.

Making pots

Greek pottery came in all shapes and sizes. Potters were skilful people who decorated their pots with beautiful designs.

Equipment

- Large margarine tubs
- Wallpaper paste
- Paper towels (cut into strips)
- Paint (orange and black)
- Paint brushes
- Thin card (cut into sections 2cm x 4cm)
- Black felt pens (different sizes)

1. Cover a tub with strips of paper towels soaked in wallpaper paste. Use many overlapping layers. Leave to dry. Remove the tub when dry. Cover the bottom of the tub.

2. Do the same thing with another tub to make the top section of the pot. Leave to dry. Remove the tub when dry. Do not cover the bottom of the tub.

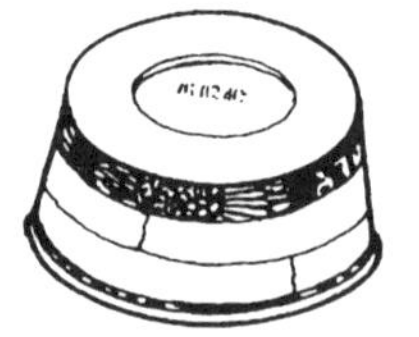

3. Stick the two tubs together using more paper towels soaked in paste.

4. Curl the pieces of thin card and paste them closely together around the top of the pot. Cover the pieces of card with more paper towels soaked in paste. Leave to dry.

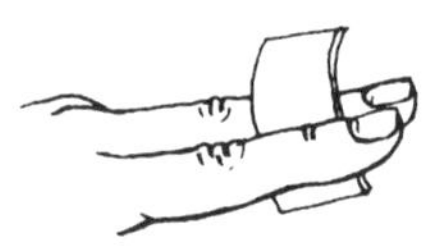

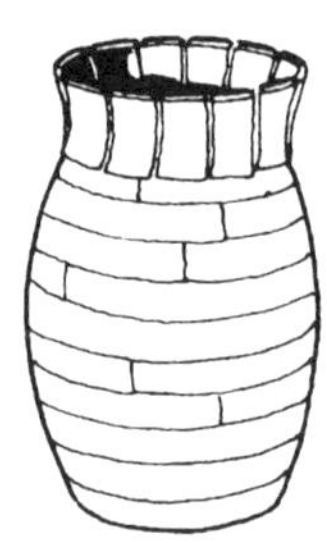

5. Cover the pot with several coats of orange paint. Leave to dry.

6. Design a decoration and draw it in pencil on the pot. Trace over the design with black felt tip pen. Use the design ideas below to help you.

- Make some pots to show everyday life in Ancient Greece. You could use some of the design ideas shown here.
- Label the pots and arrange them in a display.

Statues

1. The sculptor uses clay to make a rough shape of the statue.

2. He covers the clay with wax and then carves out the fine details.

3. The carved wax is covered in clay. The statue is then heated in an oven. The clay becomes hard, but the wax becomes soft and melts away.

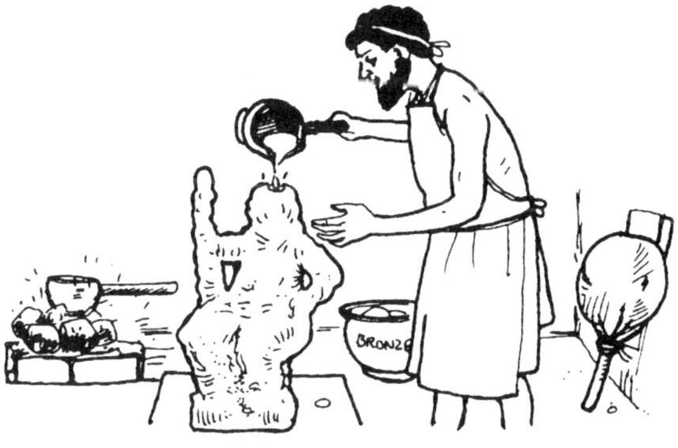

4. The sculptor pours melted bronze into the space left by the melted wax.

5. The bronze becomes hard as it cools. The clay around the bronze is then removed.

6. The finished bronze statue is polished.

Ancient Greeks used statues to decorate their buildings and public places. Many statues were made to honour their gods and goddesses. They were usually made from terracotta, marble or bronze.

- Imagine that you are a television reporter making a programme about how bronze statues were made in Ancient Greece. Write about what is happening.
- Collect and display sketches or photographs of statues in your area. Compare them to pictures of statues from Ancient Greece and write a list of the similarities and differences.

Music

Music was an important part of Ancient Greek life. It was taught at school and tunes were passed down through generations. The Ancient Greeks believed that music could change the way people thought and acted. Unfortunately, today we know very little about the music of Ancient Greece.

- Make a mobile. Cut out each card and colour it in using terracotta, black and white.
- On the back of each card, draw, colour and label a similar instrument used today.
- Add some decoration to your mobile.

Athens and Rome

When Athens was at the height of its powers in about 430BC, Rome was a small town on the banks of the Tiber. A few hundred years later, Rome was a huge city with over one million people.

ROME		✔ or ✗		ATHENS
Gods and temples The Romans thought that the gods controlled their lives. They built many temples to them.		✔		**Gods and temples** The Greeks thought that the gods controlled their lives. They built many temples to them.
Houses Most Romans lived in crowded blocks of flats called 'insulae'. Wealthy people lived in fine houses with many rooms and a courtyard.				**Houses**
Theatre Theatres were open-air, semi-circular and made from stone. Comedy and tragedy were the most popular types of play.				**Theatre**
Slaves Most slaves were captured in battles and made to work in houses, on the land or in mines. They were bought and sold in the market place.				**Slaves**
Baths Roman towns had many bath houses. People went there not only to wash but also to meet friends.				**Baths**
Sport Sport was held in the amphitheatre. Here armed slaves fought each other until one of them died. Sometimes they fought wild animals.				**Sport**
Markets The Forum was the most important part of the city. It was the market place and meeting place.				**Markets**

- Do some research. Write some details about Ancient Athens and draw some pictures. If the details are similar to Ancient Rome, tick the middle box. If they are different, draw a cross. If some things are the same put a tick and a cross.
- Describe the similarities and differences between Rome and Athens.

The Trojan War

A famous story from Ancient Greece tells how Greek soldiers, led by Agamemnon, attacked the city of Troy. They wanted to rescue Helen, who was married to Agamemnon's brother. The war lasted for ten years until a wooden horse was used to trick the people of Troy.

The Greeks built the wooden horse, hid some soldiers inside it and took it to Troy. The people of Troy took the horse inside the city gates because they thought it would bring them luck. Later that night, while the people were asleep, the soldiers crept out of the horse, unlocked the city gates and let in the Greek army that was waiting outside. The city of Troy was defeated.

Many artists have drawn the Trojan horse. Here are copies of three of them.

- How are the horses different?
- Which drawing do you think looks most like the actual Trojan Horse? Why?
- Do some research into the Trojan War. Tell the story of the war as if you were a Trojan and then tell it again as if you were a Greek. What is different about the two stories?

The Battle of Salamis

From 500BC to 449BC the Greek city states and the empire of Persia were at war. One of the largest battles of the war was the Battle of Salamis.

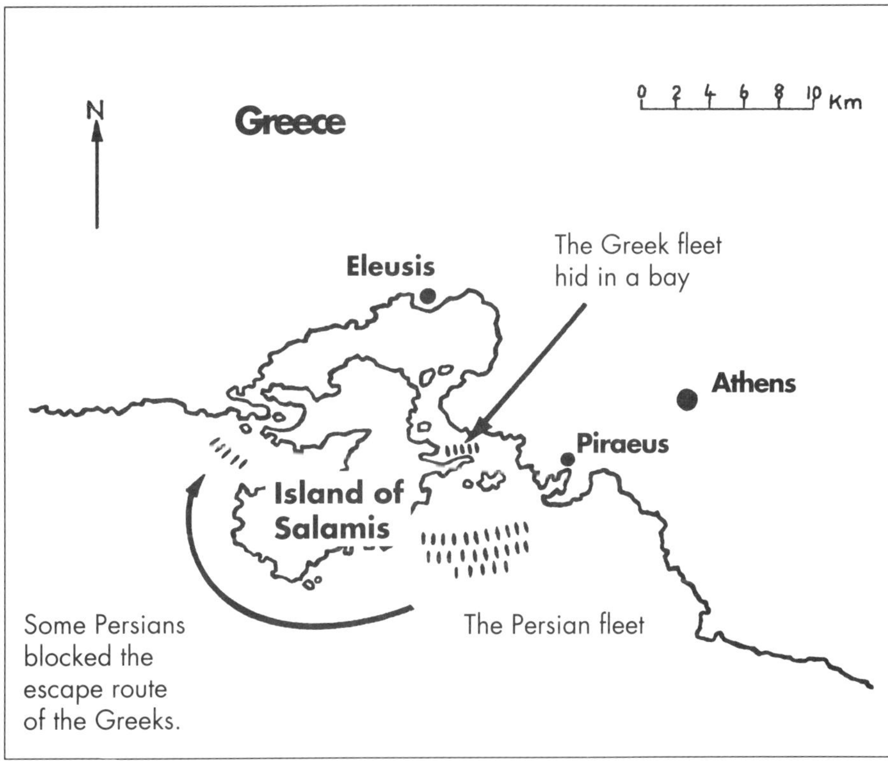

This map shows where the Battle of Salamis took place.

A painting called *The Battle of Salamis*.

- Do some research and tell the story of the Battle of Salamis in your own words. Use the information on this page to help you.
- Look carefully at the map. Why did the Greek ships hide in the bay?
- Why did some Persian ships try to block the Greeks' escape route?
- Describe carefully what is shown in the painting.
- Do you think this is really how the battle looked? Give reasons for your answer.
- Collect some pictures and information about the Battle of Salamis and make a display.

Triremes

Greek warships were called triremes. They were rowed by 170 men seated in three rows above each other. On the front of the the ship was a sharp piece of metal. The idea was to ram this into the enemy ship and sink it.

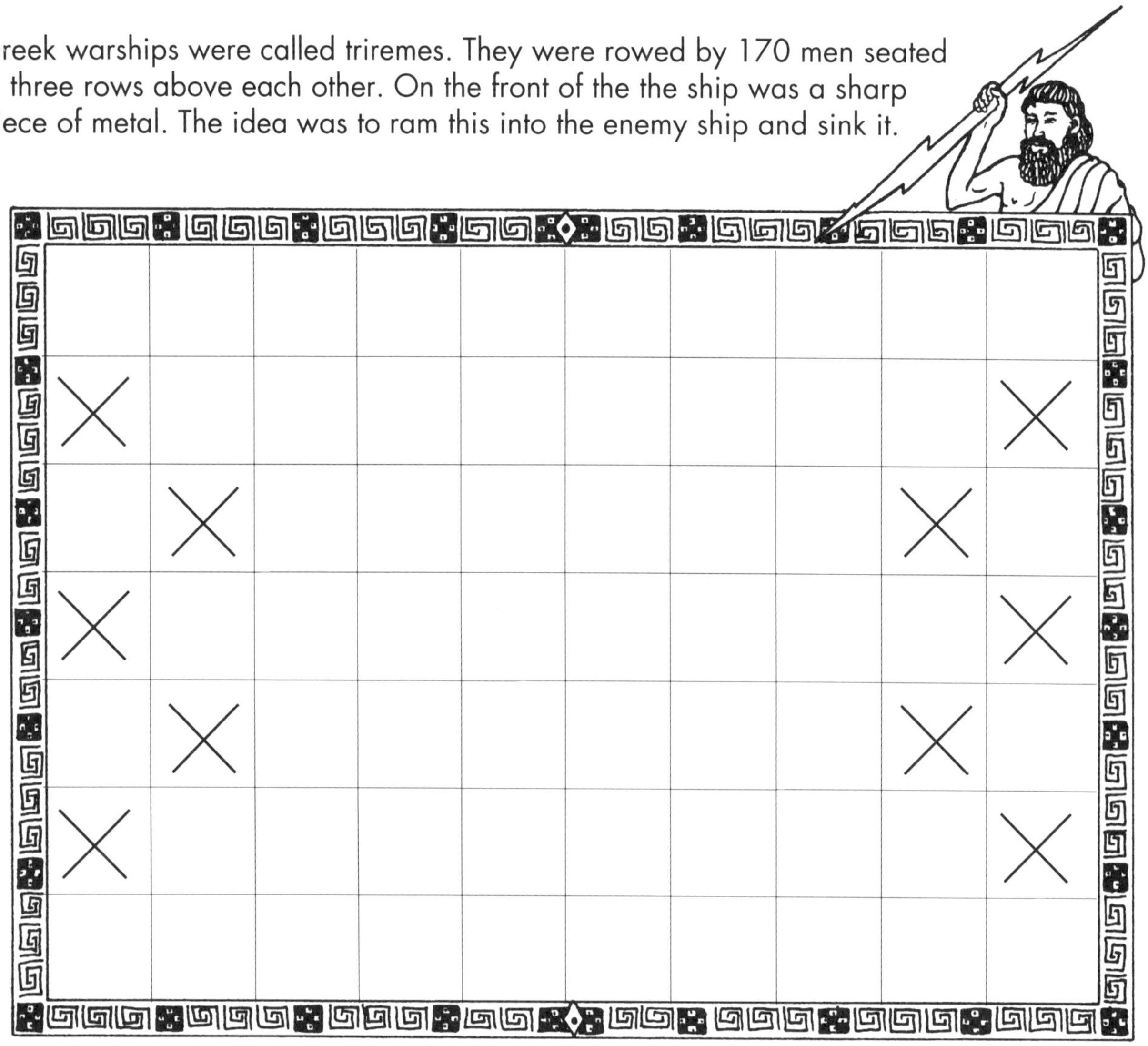

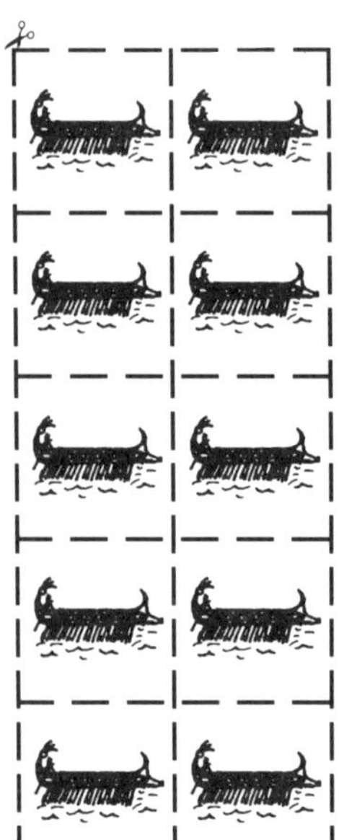

- This is a game for two players. You will need five counters each and a dice. Cut out ten counters and colour five of them blue (for the Greek triremes) and five of them red (for the Persian triremes).
- The players sit at opposite sides of the board and each player places their counters on the squares with crosses.
- Each player rolls the dice and moves a counter the correct number of spaces. Counters can be moved up or down, left or right, or diagonally.
- The aim of the game is for each player to sink the other player's triremes by ramming them. If you land on a square that contains the other player's trireme, that trireme is sunk and you take over the square.
- The winner of the game is the first player to sink all of the other player's triremes.

The Olympic Games were first held in 776BC. They took place in June or July and lasted for five days. The games were part of a competition between cities in Ancient Greece and were very popular.

- Look at the poster. Describe what is happening in each picture and add a caption to each.
- Find out more about the Olympic Games in Ancient Greece. Make a frieze showing all the different Ancient Greek Olympic events.
- Complete a chart to show the similarities and differences between the Olympic Games in Ancient Greece and today.

The Greek alphabet

The Greek alphabet was very similar to our own. Many of the letters we use today come from the Ancient Greeks. The work 'alphabet' itself is made from the first two letters of the Greek alphabet – 'alpha' and 'beta'.

modern letter	A	B	G	D	E (short)	Z	E (long)	Th	I	K	L	M	N
Greek letter	Α	Β	Γ	Δ	Ε	Ζ	Η	Θ	Ι	Κ	Λ	Μ	Ν
modern letter	X	O (short)	P	R	S	T	U	Ph, F		Kh, Ch		Ps	O (long)
Greek letter	Ξ	Ο	Π	Ρ	Σ	Τ	Υ	Φ		Χ		Ψ	Ω

Α alpha	Β beta	Γ gamma	Δ delta	Ε epsilon	Ζ zeta
Η eta	Θ theta	Ι iota	Κ kappa	Λ lambda	Μ mu
Ν nu	Ξ xi	Ο omicron	Π pi	Ρ rho	Σ sigma
Τ tau	Υ upsilon	Φ phi	Χ chi	Ψ psi	Ω omega

- The Greek Letter Game can be played by two to four players.
- Cut out the Greek letter cards, then make some letter cards for the modern English alphabet and cut them out.
- Shuffle the two sets of cards, then put the Greek cards face down in the middle and give each player six English cards.
- Turn over the Greek cards one by one. If one of the players has the same letter in their English cards, they should place it on top. The winner is the player to get rid of all their cards first.
- This game uses the capital letters of the Greek alphabet. Find out about the lower case letters and make your own game.

Democracy

Many city states in Ancient Greece introduced democracy. Athens introduced a government run by mass meetings, a legal system and elections to the councils.

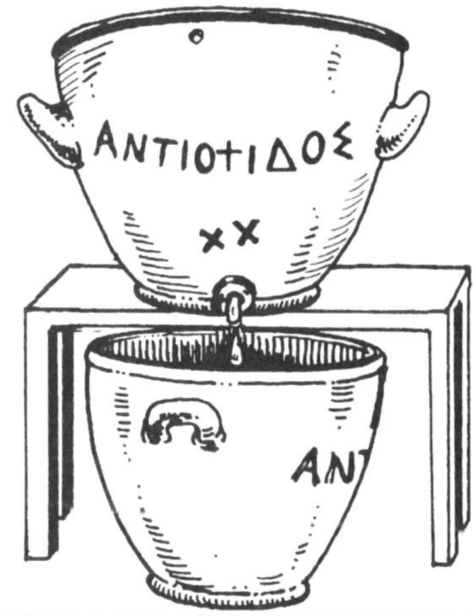

Speakers in Athenian law courts were given a fixed time for their speeches. Time was measured by a water clock.

Pericles was a member of the 'strategos'. These ten citizens, elected every year, were the political and military leaders.

Government was by mass meeting. Every citizen could attend, speak and vote. The city was governed by the votes of the crowd.

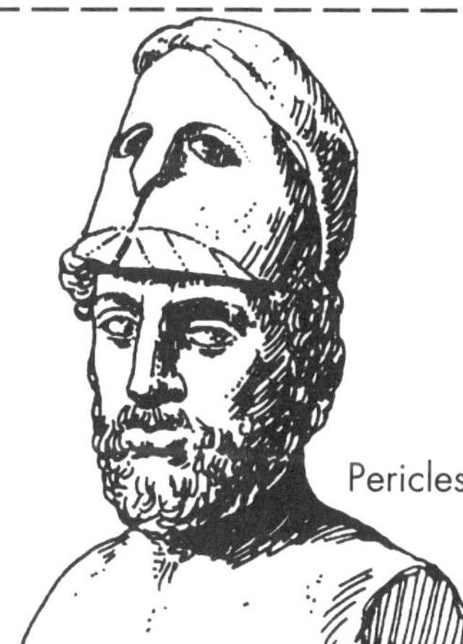

Laws were recorded for anyone to read. Hundreds of people made up a jury. Guilty and not guilty verdicts were shown by discs.

Citizens could banish a politician who was unpopular. If more than 6000 votes were cast he had to leave Athens for ten years.

The Council arranged business for the assembly. 500 paid council members were chosen by lottery. It met in the 'tholos'.

- Cut out the pictures and match them with the correct captions.
- What are the advantages and disadvantages of holding mass meetings?
- Do some research, then look at each picture carefully.
  What are the main differences and similarities with governments today?

Greece ≈ then and now

The modern world contains many things that were passed on by the Ancient Greeks. Here are just a few:

- coins
- government
- mathematics
- astronomy
- theatre
- medicine
- architecture
- words
- clocks
- law
- geography
- art

- The illustration on this page shows a modern Olympic Games. Draw pictures of some more sports and make a display.
- Choose one of the themes in the list, then investigate it and make your own display.
- Do some research and describe carefully how the modern world has benefited from the Ancient Greeks.

